Jesus of Nazareth

The Easter Message

Compiled from the text of the
Good News Bible and with illustrations from the
Lew Grade/Franco Zeffirelli film
"Jesus of Nazareth"

Photographs by Paul Ronald

The photographs were previously reproduced in
Jesus of Nazareth by William Barclay,
published by Collins

COLLINS
ST JAMES'S PLACE, LONDON
1978

Jesus is welcomed into Jerusalem

As Jesus and his disciples approached Jerusalem, they came to Bethphage at the Mount of Olives. There Jesus sent two of the disciples on ahead with these instructions: "Go to the village there ahead of you, and at once you will find a donkey tied up with her colt beside her. Untie them and bring them to me. And if anyone says anything, tell him, 'The Master needs them'; and then he will let them go at once."

This happened in order to make what the prophet had said come true:
"Tell the city of Zion,
Look, your king is coming to you!
He is humble and rides on a donkey
and on a colt, the foal of a donkey."

So the disciples went and did what Jesus had told them to do: they brought the donkey and the colt, threw their cloaks over them, and Jesus got on. A large crowd of people spread their cloaks on the road while others cut branches from the trees and spread them on the road. The crowds walking in front of Jesus and those walking behind began to shout, "Praise to David's Son! God bless him who comes in the name of the Lord! Praise God!"

When Jesus entered Jerusalem, the whole city was thrown into an uproar. "Who is he?" the people asked.

"This is the prophet Jesus, from Nazareth in Galilee," the crowds answered.

Matthew 21, 1–11

Jesus goes into the Temple

When they arrived in Jerusalem, Jesus went to the Temple and began to drive out all those who were buying and selling. He overturned the tables of the money-changers and the stools of those who sold pigeons, and he would not let anyone carry anything through the temple courtyards. He then taught the people: "It is written in the Scriptures that God said, 'My Temple will be called a house of prayer for the people of all nations.' But you have turned it into a hideout for thieves!"

The chief priests and the teachers of the Law heard of this, so they began looking for some way to kill Jesus. They were afraid of him, because the whole crowd was amazed at his teaching.

Mark 11, 15–18

He starts teaching in the Temple

Every day Jesus taught in the Temple. The chief priests, the teachers of the Law, and the leaders of the people wanted to kill him, but they could not find a way to do it, because all the people kept listening to him, not wanting to miss a single word.

Luke 19, 47–48

The blind and the crippled came to him in the Temple, and he healed them. The chief priests and the teachers of the Law became angry when they saw the wonderful things he was doing and the children shouting in the Temple. "Praise to David's Son!" So they asked Jesus, "Do you hear what they are saying?"

"Indeed I do," answered Jesus. "Haven't you ever read this scripture? 'You have trained children and babies to offer perfect praise.'"

Matthew 21, 14–15

Judas plans to betray Jesus

The time was near for the Festival of Unleavened Bread, which is called the Passover. The chief priests and the teachers of the Law were afraid of the people, and so they were trying to find a way of putting Jesus to death secretly.

Luke 22, 1–2

So the Pharisees and the chief priests met with the Council and said, "What shall we do? Look at all the miracles this man is performing! If we let him go on in this way, everyone will believe in him, and the Roman authorities will take action and destroy our Temple and our nation!"

John 11, 47–48

Then Satan entered Judas, called Iscariot, who was one of the twelve disciples. So Judas went off and spoke with the chief priests and the officers of the temple guard about how he could betray Jesus to them. They were pleased and offered to pay him money. Judas agreed to it and started looking for a good chance to hand Jesus over to them without the people knowing about it.

Luke 22, 3–6

On the first day of the Festival of Unleavened Bread the disciples came to Jesus and asked him, "Where do you want us to get the Passover meal ready for you?"
"Go to a certain man in the city," he said to them, "and tell him: 'The Teacher says, My hour has come; my disciples and I will celebrate the Passover at your house.'"
The disciples did as Jesus had told them and prepared the Passover meal.

Matthew 26, 17–19

The Last Supper

When the hour came, Jesus took his place at the table with the apostles. He said to them, "I have wanted so much to eat this Passover meal with you before I suffer! For I tell you, I will never eat it until it is given its full meaning in the Kingdom of God."

Then Jesus took a cup, gave thanks to God, and said, "Take this and share it among yourselves. I tell you that from now on I will not drink this wine until the Kingdom of God comes."

Then he took a piece of bread, gave thanks to God, broke it, and gave it to them, saying, "This is my body, which is given for you. Do this in memory of me." In the

same way, he gave them the cup after the supper, saying, "This cup is God's new covenant sealed with my blood, which is poured out for you.

"But, look! The one who betrays me is here at the table with me! The Son of Man will die as God has decided, but how terrible for that man who betrays him!"

Then they began to ask among themselves which one of them it could be who was going to do this.

Luke 22, 14–23

The agony in the garden

Then Jesus went with his disciples to a place called Gethsemane, and he said to them, "Sit here while I go over there and pray." He took with him Peter and the two sons of Zebedee. Grief and anguish came over him, and he said to them, "The sorrow in my heart is so great that it almost crushes me. Stay here and keep watch with me."

He went a little farther on, threw himself face downwards on the ground, and prayed, "My Father, if it is possible, take this cup of suffering from me! Yet not what I want, but what you want."

Then he returned to the three disciples and found them asleep; and he said to Peter, "How is it that you three were not able to keep watch with me even for one hour? Keep watch and pray that you will not fall into temptation. The spirit is willing, but the flesh is weak."

Once more Jesus went away and prayed, "My Father, if this cup of suffering cannot be taken away unless I drink it, your will be done." He returned once more and found the disciples asleep; they could not keep their eyes open.

Again Jesus left them, went away, and prayed the third time, saying the same words. Then he returned to the disciples and said, "Are you still sleeping and resting? Look! The hour has come for the Son of Man to be handed over to the power of sinful men. Get up, let us go. Look, here is the man who is betraying me!"

Matthew 26, 36–46

The arrest of Jesus

Jesus was still speaking when Judas, one of the twelve disciples, arrived. With him was a large crowd armed with swords and clubs and sent by the chief priests and the elders. The traitor had given the crowd a signal: "The man I kiss is the one you want.

Judas went straight to Jesus and said, "Peace be with you, Teacher," and kissed him.

Jesus is put on trial

Those who had arrested Jesus took him to the house of Caiaphas, the High Priest, where the teachers of the Law and the elders had gathered together. Peter followed from a distance, as far as the courtyard of the High Priest's house. He went into the courtyard and sat down with the guards to see how it would all come out. The chief priests and the whole Council tried to find some false evidence against Jesus to put him to death; but they could not find any, even though many people came forward and told lies about him. Finally two men stepped up and said, "This man said, 'I am able to tear down God's Temple and three days later build it up again.'"

The High Priest stood up and said to Jesus, "Have you no answer to give to this accusation against you?" But Jesus kept quiet. Again the High Priest spoke to him, "In the name of the living God I now put you on oath: tell us if you are the Messiah, the Son of God."

Jesus answered him, "So you say. But I tell all of you: from this time on you will see the Son of Man sitting on the right of the Almighty and coming on the clouds of heaven!"

At this the High Priest tore his clothes and said, "Blasphemy! We don't need any more witnesses! You have just heard his blasphemy! What do you think?"

They answered, "He is guilty and must die."

Matthew 26, 57–66

Peter and Judas

Peter was sitting outside in the courtyard when one of the High Priest's servant-girls came to him and said, "You, too, were with Jesus of Galilee."

But he denied it in front of them all. "I don't know what you are talking about," he answered, and went on out to the entrance of the courtyard. Another servant-girl saw him and said to the men there, "He was with Jesus of Nazareth."

Again Peter denied it and answered, "I swear that I don't know that man!"

After a little while the men standing there came to Peter. "Of course you are one of them," they said. "After all, the way you speak gives you away!"

Then Peter said, "I swear that I am telling the truth! May God punish me if I am not! I do not know that man!"

Just then a cock crowed and Peter remembered what Jesus had told him: "Before the cock crows, you will say three times that you do not know me." He went out and wept bitterly.

Matthew 26, 69–75

When Judas, the traitor, learnt that Jesus had been condemned, he repented and took back the thirty silver coins to the chief priests and the elders. "I have sinned by betraying an innocent man to death!" he said.

"What do we care about that?" they answered. "That is your business!"

Judas threw the coins down in the Temple and left; then he went off and hanged himself.

Matthew 27, 3–5

"What is truth?"

Early in the morning all the chief priests and the elders made their plans against Jesus to put him to death. They put him in chains, led him off, and handed him over to Pilate, the Roman governor.

Matthew 27, 1–2

Jesus stood before the Roman governor, who questioned him. "Are you the king of the Jews?" he asked.

"So you say," answered Jesus. But he said nothing in response to the accusations of the chief priests and elders.

So Pilate said to him, "Don't you hear all these things they accuse you of?"

Matthew 27, 11–13

Jesus said, "My kingdom does not belong to this world; if my kingdom belonged to this world, my followers would fight to keep me from being handed over to the Jewish authorities. No, my kingdom does not belong here!"

So Pilate asked him, "Are you a king, then?"

Jesus answered, "You say that I am a king. I was born and came into the world for this one purpose, to speak about the truth. Whoever belongs to the truth listens to me."

"And what is truth?" Pilate asked.

John 18, 36–38

The crown of thorns

Then Pilate's soldiers took Jesus into the governor's palace, and the whole company gathered round him. They stripped off his clothes and put a scarlet robe on him. Then they made a crown out of thorny branches and placed it on his head, and put a stick in his right hand; then they knelt before him and mocked him. "Long live the King of the Jews!" they said.

Matthew 27, 27–29

The crowd condemns Jesus

At every Passover Festival the Roman governor was in the habit of setting free any one prisoner the crowd asked for. At that time there was a well-known prisoner named Jesus Barabbas. So when the crowd gathered, Pilate asked them, "Which one do you want me to set free for you? Jesus Barabbas or Jesus called the Messiah?" He knew very well that the Jewish authorities had handed Jesus over to him because they were jealous.

While Pilate was sitting in the judgement hall, his wife sent him a message: "Have nothing to do with that innocent man, because in a dream last night I suffered much on account of him."

The chief priests and the elders persuaded the crowd to ask Pilate to set Barabbas free and have Jesus put to death. But Pilate asked the crowd, "Which one of these two do you want me to set free for you?"
"Barabbas!" they answered.
"What, then, shall I do with Jesus called the Messiah?" Pilate asked them.
"Crucify him!" they all answered.
But Pilate asked, "What crime has he committed?"
Then they started shouting at the top of their voices: "Crucify him!"
When Pilate saw that it was no use to go on, but that a riot might break out, he took some water, washed his hands in front of the crowd, and said, "I am not responsible for the death of this man! This is your doing!"

Matthew 27, 15—24

Jesus is crucified

So they took charge of Jesus. He went out, carrying his cross, and came to "The Place of the Skull," as it is called. (In Hebrew it is called "Golgotha.")

John 19, 16b–17

Two other men, both of them criminals, were also led out to be put to death with Jesus. When they came to the place called "The Skull," they crucified Jesus there, and the two criminals, one on his right and the other on his left. Jesus said, "Forgive them, Father! They don't know what they are doing." They divided his clothes among themselves by throwing dice.

The people stood there watching while the Jewish leaders jeered at him: "He saved others; let him save himself if he is the Messiah whom God has chosen!"

The soldiers also mocked him; they came up to him and offered him cheap wine, and said, "Save yourself if you are the king of the Jews!"

Above him were written these words: "This is the King of the Jews."

One of the criminals hanging there hurled insults at him: "Aren't you the Messiah? Save yourself and us!"

The other one, however, rebuked him, saying "Don't you fear God? You received the same sentence he did. Ours, however, is only right, because we are getting what we deserve for what we did; but he has done no wrong." And he said to Jesus, "Remember me, Jesus, when you come as King!"

Jesus said to him, "I promise you that today you will be in Paradise with me."

Luke 23, 32–43

"It is finished!"

Standing close to Jesus' cross were his mother, his mother's sister, Mary the wife of Clopas, and Mary Magdalene. Jesus saw his mother and the disciple he loved standing there; so he said to his mother, "He is your son."

Then he said to the disciple, "She is your mother." From that time the disciple took her to live in his home.

Jesus knew that by now everything had been completed; and in order to make the scripture come true, he said, "I am thirsty."

A bowl was there, full of cheap wine; so a sponge was soaked in the wine, put on a stalk of hyssop, and lifted up to his lips. Jesus drank the wine and said, "It is finished!"

Then he bowed his head and died.

John 19, 25–30

"Jesus is alive!"

There was a man named Joseph from Arimathea, a town in Judaea. He was a good and honourable man, who was waiting for the coming of the Kingdom of God. Although he was a member of the Council, he had not agreed with their decision and action. He went into the presence of Pilate and asked for the body of Jesus. Then he took the body down, wrapped it in a linen sheet, and placed it in a tomb which had been dug out of solid rock and which had never been used. It was Friday, and the Sabbath was about to begin.

On the Sabbath they rested, as the Law commanded.

Luke 23, 50–56

Early on Sunday morning, while it was still dark, Mary Magdalene went to the tomb and saw that the stone had been taken away from the entrance. She went running to Simon Peter and the other disciple, whom Jesus loved, and told them, "They have taken the Lord from the tomb, and we don't know where they have put him!"

Mary stood crying outside the tomb. While she was still crying, she bent over and looked in the tomb and saw two angels there dressed in white, sitting where the body of Jesus had been, one at the head and the other at the feet. "Woman, why are you crying?" they asked her.

She answered, "They have taken my Lord away, and I do not know where they have put him!"

Then she turned round and saw Jesus standing there; but she did not know that it was Jesus. "Woman, why are you crying?" Jesus asked her. "Who is it that you are looking for?"

She thought he was the gardener, so she said to him, "If you took him away, sir, tell me where you have put him, and I will go and get him."

Jesus said to her, "Mary!"

She turned towards him and said in Hebrew, "Rabboni!" (This means "Teacher.")

"Do not hold on to me," Jesus told her, "because I have not yet gone back up to the Father. But go to my brothers and tell them that I am returning to him who is my Father and their Father, my God and their God."

So Mary Magdalene went and told the disciples that she had seen the Lord and related to them what he had told her.

John 20, 1–2, 11–18

Jesus appears to his disciples

Last of all, Jesus appeared to the eleven disciples as they were eating. He scolded them, because they did not have faith and because they were too stubborn to believe those who had seen him alive. He said to them, "Go throughout the whole world and preach the gospel to all mankind."

Mark 16, 14–15